Seeds
and
Flowers

Written by Emily Bone

Illustrated by Samara Hardy

Designed by Zoe Wray

Flower consultant: Zoë Simmons
Reading consultant: Alison Kelly

Contents

Different shapes

There are thousands of different types of flowers growing all over the world.

Nasturtiums are trumpet-shaped with round leaves.

A dandelion flower is lots of tiny flowers clustered together.

Thistle flowers are covered in prickles.

From a seed

Flowers grow from seeds.
Seeds are tiny, young plants
packed inside hard cases.

A sunflower seed is in the soil.
The sun warms up the soil.
Then the rain makes it damp.

A root begins
to grow down.

Next a shoot grows up above the ground. Two leaves grow from the shoot.

The root grows bigger. It sucks up water from the soil.

Growing bigger

As a plant grows, it gets more leaves.
Then its leaves grow bigger.

Long stems grow and
buds appear on top.

When the buds
open, flowers
appear. These are
poppy flowers.

7

Feeding from flowers

Flowers make a sweet liquid called nectar.
Bees visit flowers to drink the nectar.

A bee lands on
a flower. It gets
covered in a dust,
called pollen, from
inside the flower.

Bees fly from flower to flower, drinking the nectar from different ones.

The bees spread the pollen around too. Flowers need pollen to grow new seeds.

Pollen spreaders

Other animals drink nectar from flowers. They help to spread pollen too.

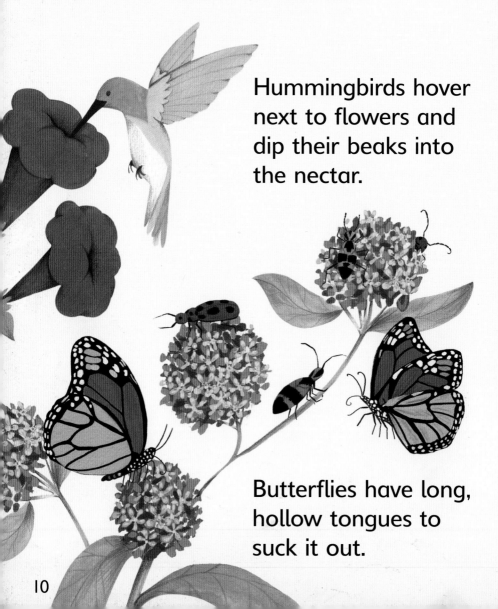

Hummingbirds hover next to flowers and dip their beaks into the nectar.

Butterflies have long, hollow tongues to suck it out.

Some flowers only
open at night. Bats
and moths visit them
to drink their nectar.

Fruitful flowers

Some flowers grow fruit when they get pollen from another flower.

The petals on a strawberry flower fall off. A small, green strawberry starts to grow.

The dots on the outside are tiny seeds.

The strawberry grows
bigger and gradually
turns red. Now it's ripe.

Birds eat the fruit.
They spread the
seeds in their
droppings.

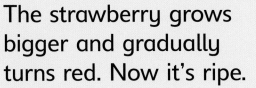

13

Tree flowers

In the spring, trees grow flowers.

Horse chestnut trees have tall flowers. Bees fly from flower to flower.

Bright red cherries
will grow from these
delicate cherry tree flowers.

Magnolia trees have
flowers with big,
open petals.

Using the wind

Some flowers don't need animals to spread their pollen.

These flowers are called catkins. They dangle from the branches of birch trees.

16

When the wind blows,
the pollen dust travels
from one catkin to another.

Growing seeds

At first, dandelions grow
bright yellow flowers.

After a couple
of days, the
petals close
up tightly.

When the flower opens again,
lots of fluffy seeds have grown.

The wind blows and
the seeds float away.

Desert flowers

In a desert, it's very hot and it hardly ever rains.

Desert plants stay alive by storing water in their spiky leaves.

Saguaro
cactus

Ocotillo

Barrel cactus

After it rains, the plants grow flowers.
Lots of flowers grow on the ground too.

Water flowers

Some flowers grow in ponds and rivers.
Their roots grow down under the water.

Pond lilies have big
flowers and wide,
waxy leaves that
float on the surface.

Water violets grow flowers on tall stems that stretch up above the water.

These unusual flowers are called bulrushes.

In a rainforest

Rainforests are warm and very rainy. They're filled with tall, bushy trees that block out the sun.

Orchids

Many flowers grow high up on branches at the tops of trees so they get lots of sunlight.

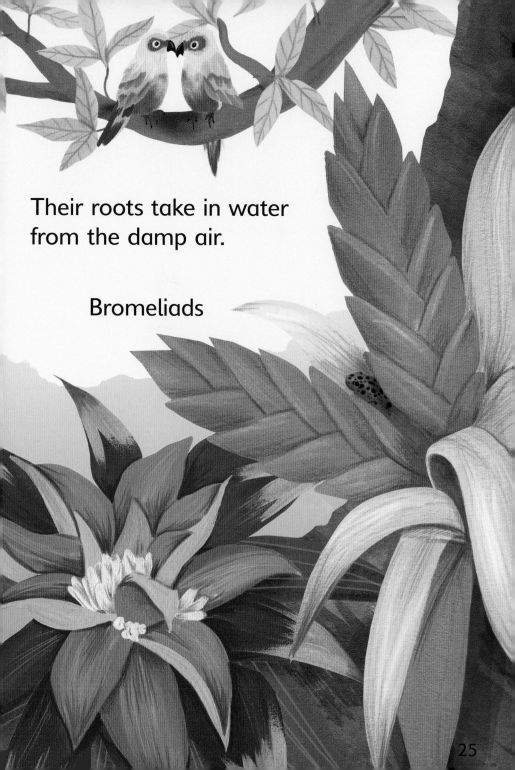

Their roots take in water
from the damp air.

Bromeliads

The biggest flower

The biggest flower in the world grows in the rainforest. It's called a rafflesia.

A rafflesia grows on the ground and can be as big as the wheel on a truck.

It smells of rotting meat. This attracts flies which help to spread its pollen.

At the end

When a flower starts to die,
its petals droop and fall off.

A poppy flower grows a pod full of seeds.
The wind blows the pod from side to side.

The seeds fall out and
down to the ground.

Eventually, they
will grow into new
poppy plants.

Glossary

Here are some of the words in this book you might not know. This page tells you what they mean.

 seed - a hard case with a tiny young plant inside.

 root - the part of a flower that sucks up water from the soil.

 shoot - a young flower, when it's just started to grow.

 bud - a flower before it has opened.

 nectar - a sweet liquid inside flowers. Animals visit flowers to drink nectar.

 pollen - a sticky dust inside flowers. Flowers need pollen to grow seeds.

 seed pod - the part of a flower where seeds grow.

Usborne Quicklinks

Would you like to discover more about how seeds and flowers grow? You can visit Usborne Quicklinks for links to exciting websites with video clips, amazing facts and ideas for fun things to make and do.

Go to **usborne.com/Quicklinks** and type in the keywords **"beginners seeds and flowers"**. Make sure you ask a grown-up before going online.

Notes for grown-ups

Please read the internet safety guidelines at the Usborne Quicklinks website with your child. Children should be supervised online. The websites are regularly reviewed and the links at Usborne Quicklinks are updated. However, Usborne Publishing is not responsible and does not accept liability for the content or availability of any website other than its own.

Sunflowers have big, bright flowers on long stems. Lots of seeds grow in the middle of a sunflower.

Index

Acknowledgements

Managing Designer: Zoe Wray

Additional design by Tabitha Blore

Digital retouching by John Russell

Sun, moon and stars

Farm animals

Elizabeth I

Rubbish & Recycling

Dogs

Horses and ponies

Spiders

Planes

Cats

Ancient Greeks

VOLCANOES

DINOSAURS

Your Body

Armour

Sharks

The Celts

VIKINGS

Castles

How flowers grow

Digging up the past

Caterpillars and Butterflies

Ballet

Pirates

EGYPTIANS

Eggs and Chicks

ROMANS

Weather

Tadpoles and frogs

Why do we eat?

Under the sea

 Bears
 AZTECS
 TRUCKS
 Night Animals
 Firefighters

 Antarctica
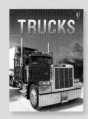 Bugs
 COWBOYS
 Planet Earth
 London

 Seashore
 China
 Dangerous Animals
 Rainforests
 Trees

 Reptiles
 Ships
 Bats
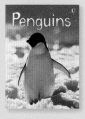 Penguins
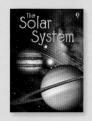 The Solar System

 Knights
 Monkeys
 Trains
 Elephants
 Tigers

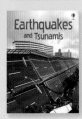 Earthquakes and Tsunamis
 Storms and Hurricanes
 Bees and Wasps
 Wolves
 Owls